BJ's Adventures... Do You Know the Continents?

Author: Tomiko Cobb

Illustrator: Ika Wahyu

Tomiko Cobb
4002 Hwy 78 W Ste. 530-211
Snellville, GA 30039
www.publishingdreamsagency.com

Do you know the continents, the continents, the continents?

Do you know the continents all around the world?

There's Africa, Asia, North America, South America, Australia, Antarctica, and Europe too!

PASSPORT

Africa
2nd Largest Continent

Sahara desert is the largest desert in the world.

The Nile River in Egypt is the longest in the world.

Africa is home to 4 of the 5 fastest land animals; which are the cheetah, lion, gazelle, and wildebeest.

Sahara desert

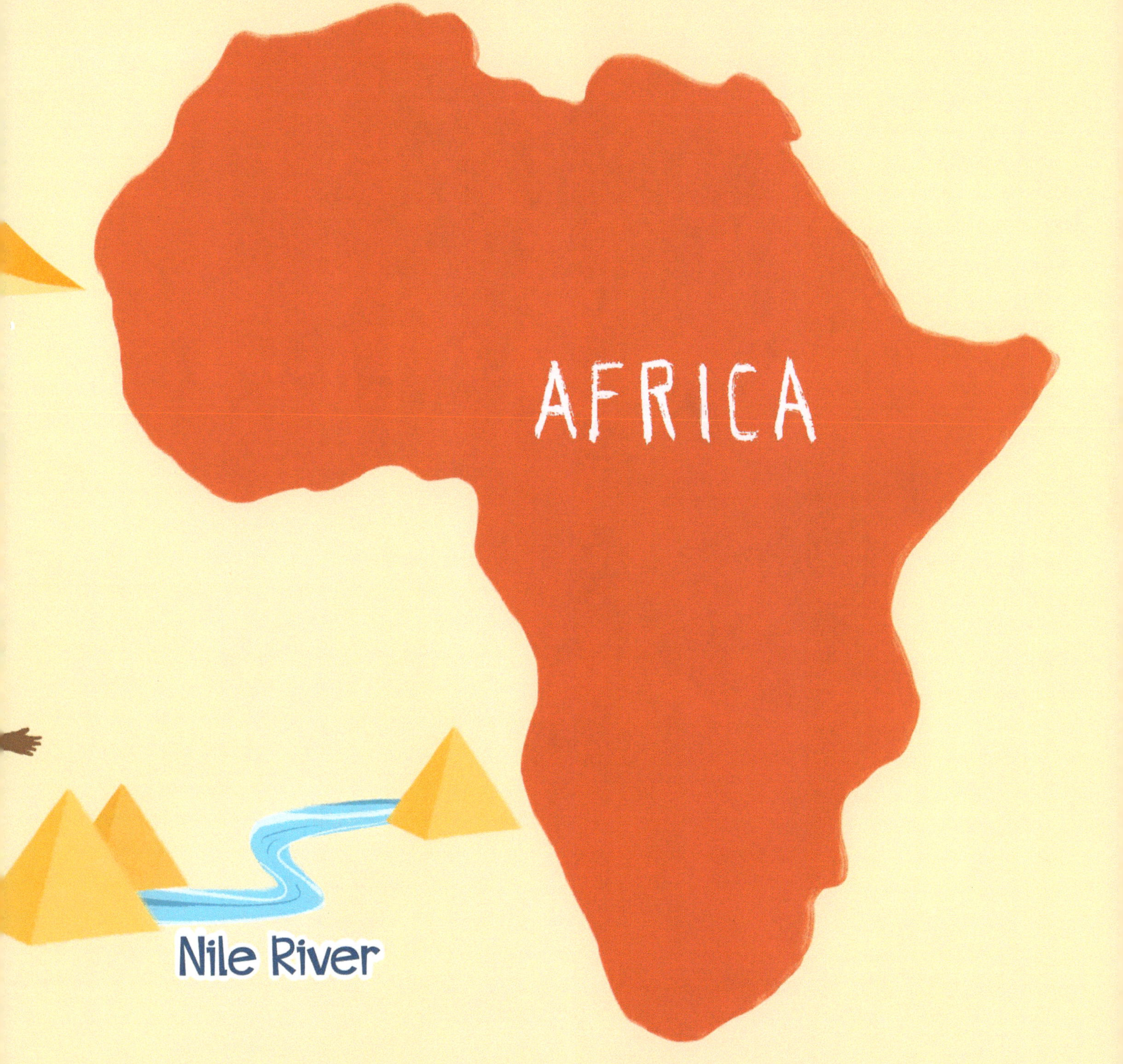
AFRICA
Nile River

ASIA

29,035 feet

Mount Everest

Asia is the largest continent. It has the most people living there.

The Great Wall of China is there!

It is home of the 10 highest mountain peaks in the world! The greatest elevation on earth is at the top of Mount Everest. (29,035 feet above sea level)

Great Wall of China

North America
3rd Largest Continent

Lake Superior is the largest freshwater lake in the world.

The Mississippi River is the 3rd largest river in the world.
Do you know what continent you live in?

That's right, it's North America!

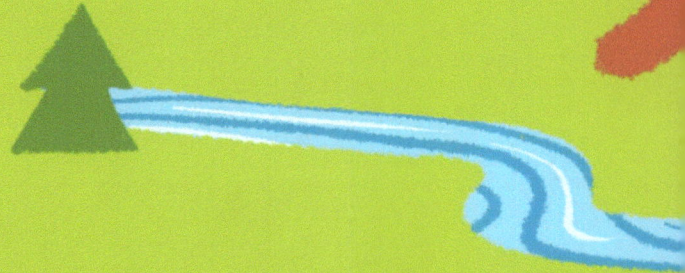

The Mississipi River

NORTH AMERICA

Lake Superior

South America
4th Largest Continent

The Andes Mountain is the 2nd highest mountain!

Mexico is in South America.

Santudel Angel is the highest waterfall in the world at 3212 feet.

The Andes Mountain

SOUTH AMERICA

Santudel Angel Waterfall

AUSTRALIA

Australia is the smallest continent in the world.

Australia has only one country, Australia.
Also known as
"The Island Continent."

It is the largest island.

Antarctica
5th largest continent

98% is covered in ice.

Is the windiest and coldest place on earth!

ANTARCTICA

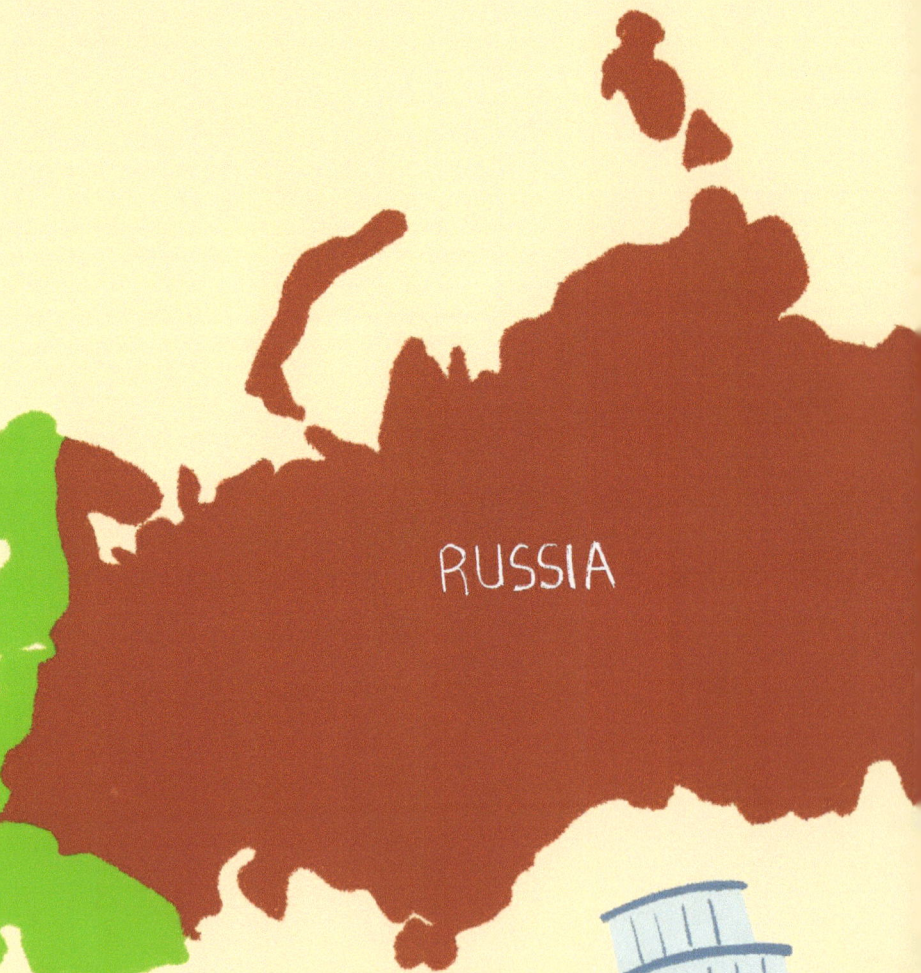

RUSSIA

EUROPE

Europe
6th largest continent

Europe has the world's largest country, Russia.

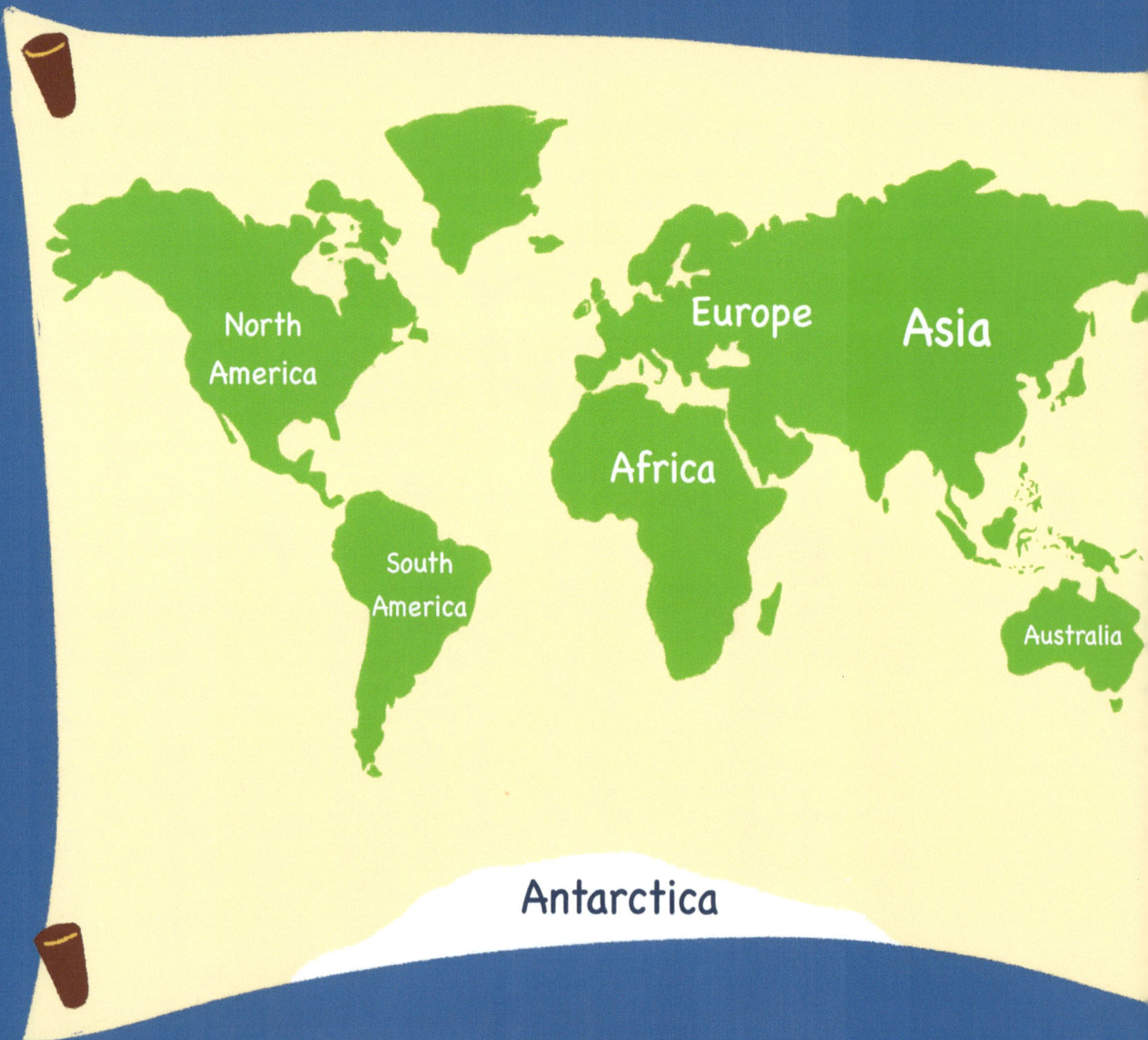

Do you know the continents, the continents, the continents?

Do you know the continents all around the world?

There's Africa, Asia, North America, South America, Australia, Antarctica, and Europe too!

GUIDING QUESTIONS:

Where do I live?

How would you describe where you live to a friend from another country?

What is a map?

What is a globe?

How are maps and globes similar and how are they different?

How is land indicated on a map or globe?

How is water indicated on a map or globe?

What makes each continent similar?

What makes each continent unique?

How do we find our way around the world?

www.ingramcontent.com/pod-product-compliance
Lightning Source LLC
Chambersburg PA
CBHW061147030426
42335CB00002B/139